Usborne
Build your own
TRUCKS
Sticker Book

Illustrated by John Shirley

Designed by Marc Maynard and Tim Ki-Kydd
Written by Simon Tudhope

Contents

Flatbed tow truck

This truck rescues cars from crash-sites and carries them to a repair shop.

Statistics

- **Size:** 23ft long
- **Loaded weight:** 9 tons
- **Horsepower:** 150hp
- **Top speed:** 70mph

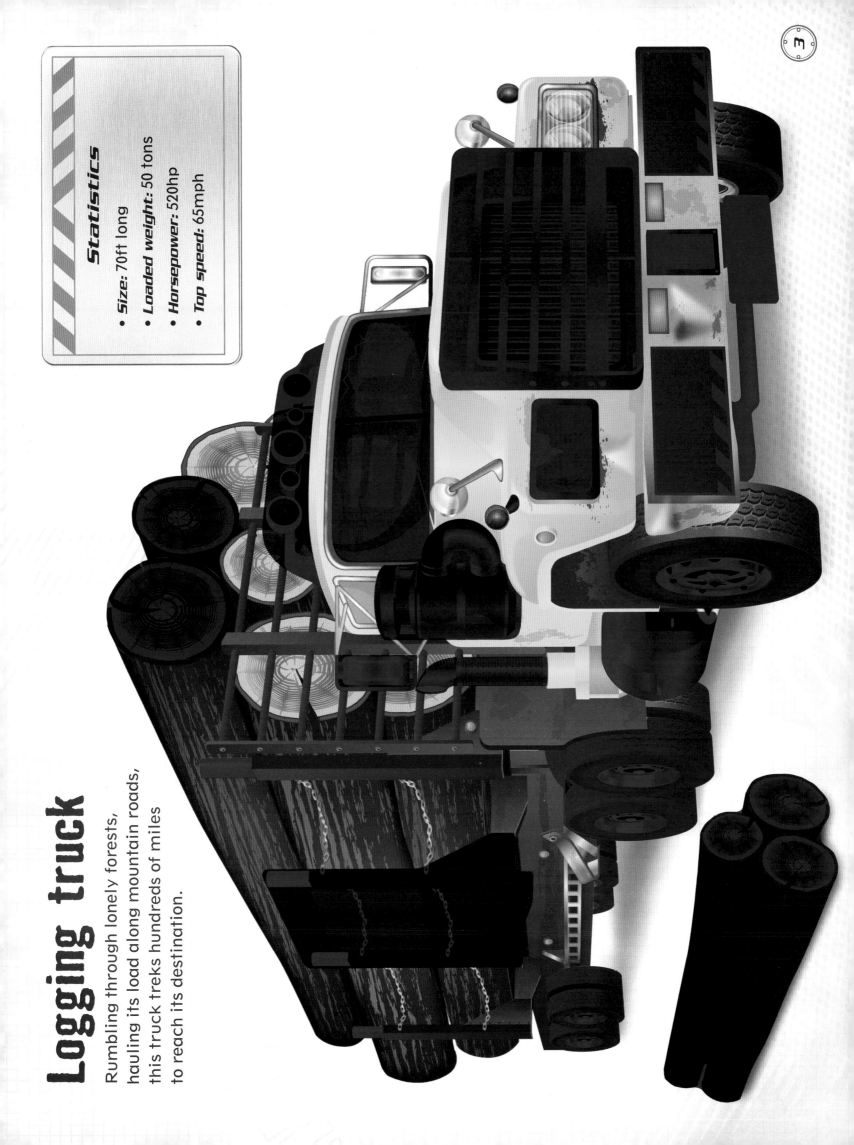

Logging truck

Rumbling through lonely forests, hauling its load along mountain roads, this truck treks hundreds of miles to reach its destination.

Statistics

- **Size:** 70ft long
- **Loaded weight:** 50 tons
- **Horsepower:** 520hp
- **Top speed:** 65mph

Armored truck

This is one of the toughest machines on four wheels. It uses armor plating and bulletproof glass to carry police through heavy gunfire.

Statistics

- **Size:** 20ft long
- **Weight:** 9 tons
- **Horsepower:** 300hp
- **Top speed:** 90mph

Construction dump truck

This steel giant can carry the weight of forty elephants.
The ground shakes as it moves through mining sites
transporting sand and gravel.

Statistics

- **Size:** 50ft long
- **Loaded weight:** 690 tons
- **Horsepower:** 4000hp
- **Top speed:** 40mph

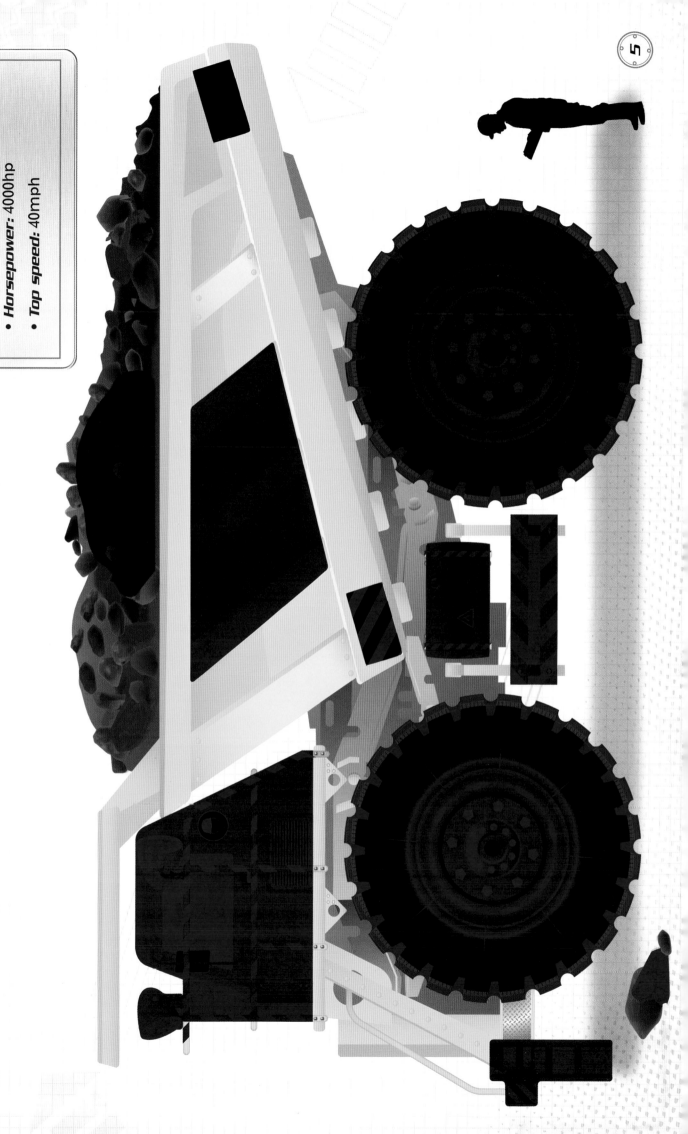

Fire truck

This truck races toward burning buildings with its lights flashing and sirens wailing. It helps battle the blaze and rescue the people inside.

Statistics

- **Size:** 30ft long
- **Loaded weight:** 18 tons
- **Horsepower:** 280hp
- **Top speed:** 70mph

Crane truck

Fitted with a strong hydraulic arm, this truck grabs its own load and lowers it to the ground.

Statistics

- **Size:** 23ft long
- **Loaded weight:** 21 tons
- **Horsepower:** 310hp
- **Top speed:** 70mph

WARNING

WARNING

Semi truck

Rolling along the open road, engine rumbling like a thundercloud, this truck covers hundreds of miles in a single day.

EAGLE HAULING

Statistics

- **Size:** 62ft long
- **Loaded weight:** 40 tons
- **Horsepower:** 600hp
- **Top speed:** 85mph

Army truck

This machine powers soldiers through tough terrain. Its double tires stop it from sinking in the mud and its engine runs on almost any fuel.

Statistics

- **Size:** 23ft long
- **Weight:** 6.5 tons
- **Horsepower:** 170hp
- **Top speed:** 60mph

Monster truck

Thundering around specially-built tracks, this supercharged beast clambers over empty cars and leaps over buses.

Statistics

- **Size:** 20ft long
- **Weight:** 5 tons
- **Horsepower:** 1500hp
- **Top speed:** 70mph

Suction excavator

Doing the dirty work that keeps our cities clean, this machine sucks up the gunk that blocks gutters and drains.

Statistics

- **Size:** 26ft long
- **Loaded weight:** 20 tons
- **Horsepower:** 200hp
- **Top speed:** 60mph

Steam truck

A hundred years ago this steam-powered truck chugged down cobbled streets, delivering coal to people's houses. It pulled up with a blast of its whistle and everyone came out to fill their sacks.

Statistics

- **Size:** 20ft long
- **Loaded weight:** 8 tons
- **Horsepower:** 90hp
- **Top speed:** 15mph

MORGAN & SONS
ESTABLISHED 1856
23

Flatbed dump truck

A builder's best friend. These dump trucks rumble around construction sites carrying huge piles of sand and gravel.

Statistics

- **Size:** 30ft long
- **Loaded weight:** 45 tons
- **Horsepower:** 340hp
- **Top speed:** 60mph

Off-road racer

Flinging thick dust clouds into the air, this truck storms around desert tracks like a mini-tornado.

Statistics

- **Size:** 16ft long
- **Weight:** 3 tons
- **Horsepower:** 750hp
- **Top speed:** 140mph

Army transporter

This truck is built for war zones. Equipped with anti-tank missiles and armor plating, it plunges through enemy territory with its cargo safe inside.

Statistics

- **Size:** 46ft long
- **Loaded weight:** 45 tons
- **Horsepower:** 500hp
- **Top speed:** 60mph

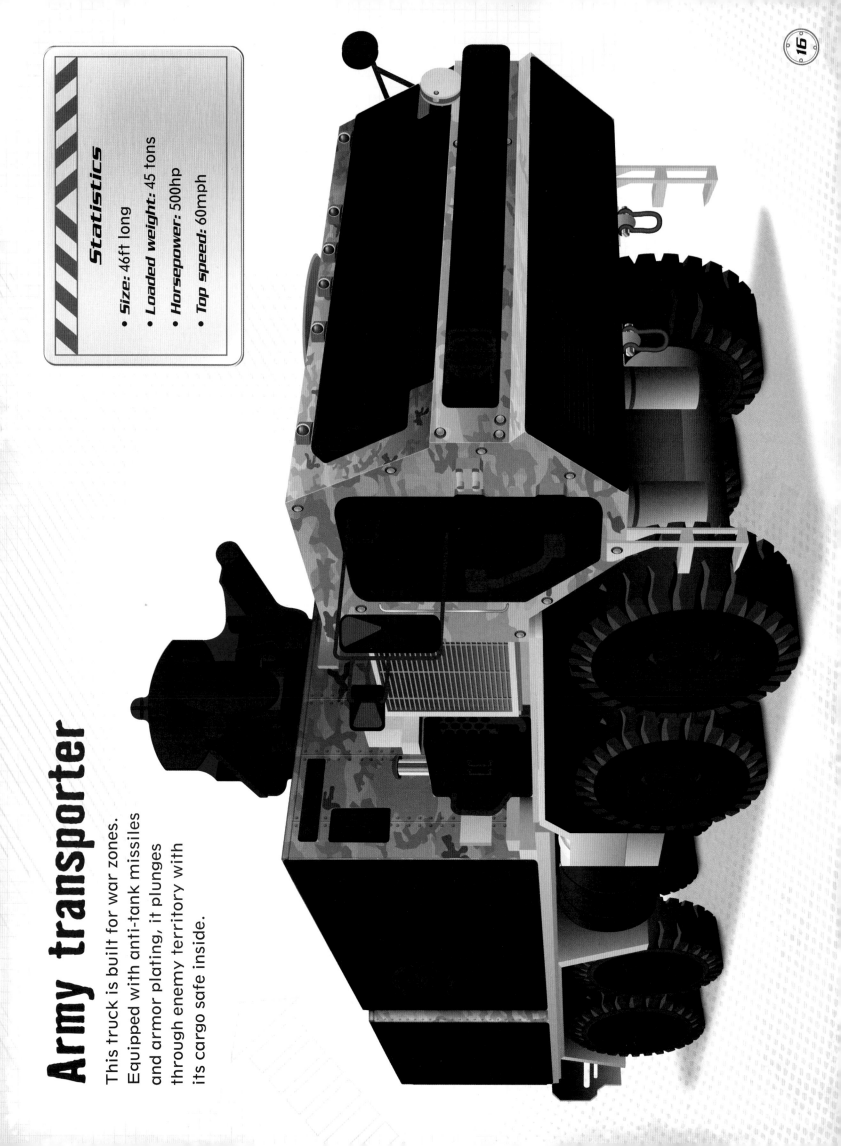

Drill truck

This machine cuts through solid rock to reach water trapped deep underground. Using a tungsten-tipped drill, it digs a well in under a day.

Statistics

- **Size:** 20ft long
- **Weight:** 11 tons
- **Horsepower:** 200hp
- **Top speed:** 55mph

Vintage pickup truck

A 1950s American classic. This truck was used by builders, farmers and anyone else who needed space in the back for the tools of their trade.

Concrete mixer

This is one of the most important machines on a building site. It churns concrete in its metal drum to stop it from setting hard.

Statistics

- **Size:** 33ft long
- **Loaded weight:** 31 tons
- **Horsepower:** 330hp
- **Top speed:** 60mph

Fuel tanker

Carrying thousands of gallons of fuel to gas stations across the country, this is the truck that keeps our cars on the move.

Statistics

- **Size:** 50ft long
- **Loaded weight:** 45 tons
- **Horsepower:** 350hp
- **Top speed:** 60mph

Pro-jet truck

The loudest, fastest, most insane truck on the planet. With engines from a jet plane strapped to its back, it blasts down tire-scorched dragstrips.

Statistics

- **Size:** 23ft long
- **Weight:** 3.5 tons
- **Horsepower:** 36000hp
- **Top speed:** 375mph

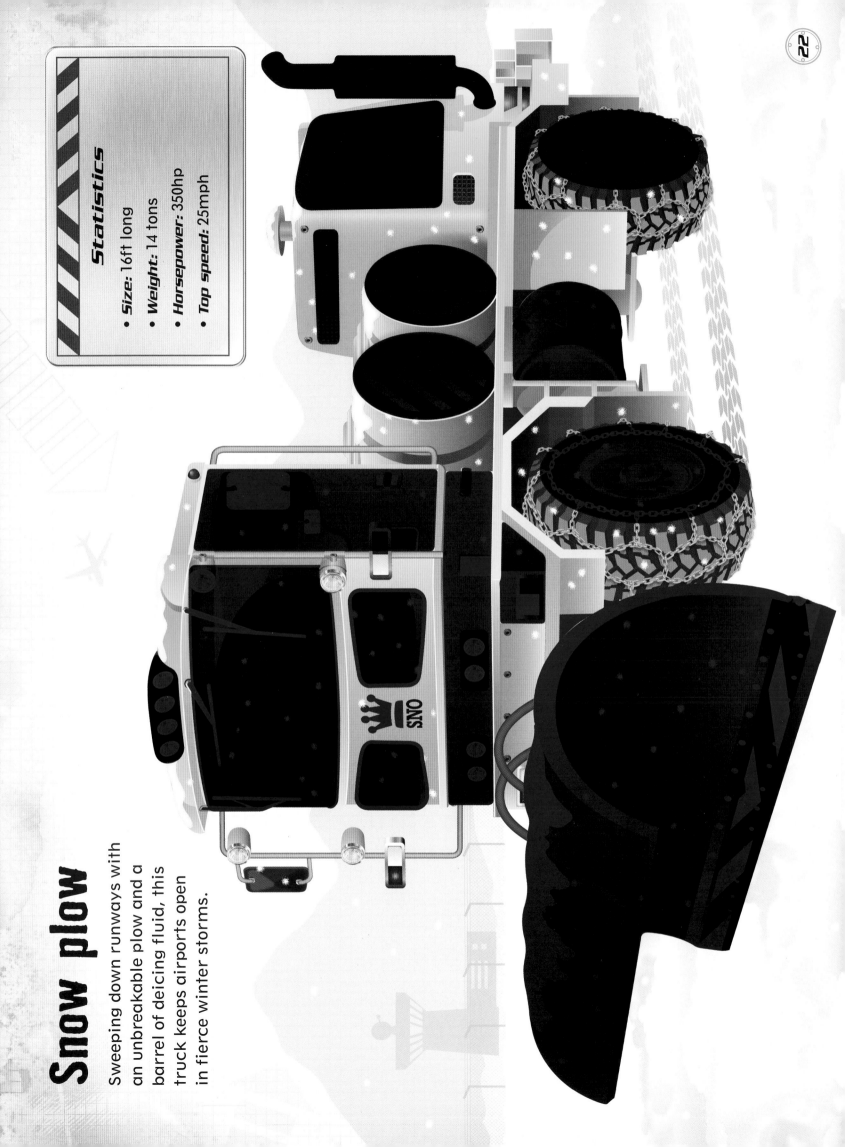

Snow plow

Sweeping down runways with an unbreakable plow and a barrel of deicing fluid, this truck keeps airports open in fierce winter storms.

Statistics

- **Size:** 16ft long
- **Weight:** 14 tons
- **Horsepower:** 350hp
- **Top speed:** 25mph

Ballast tractor

Towing a boat along a road takes a special machine. With a purpose-built engine for huge pulling power at low speeds, this is the truck for the job.

Statistics

- **Size:** 100ft long
- **Loaded weight:** 200 tons
- **Horsepower:** 650hp
- **Top speed:** 30mph

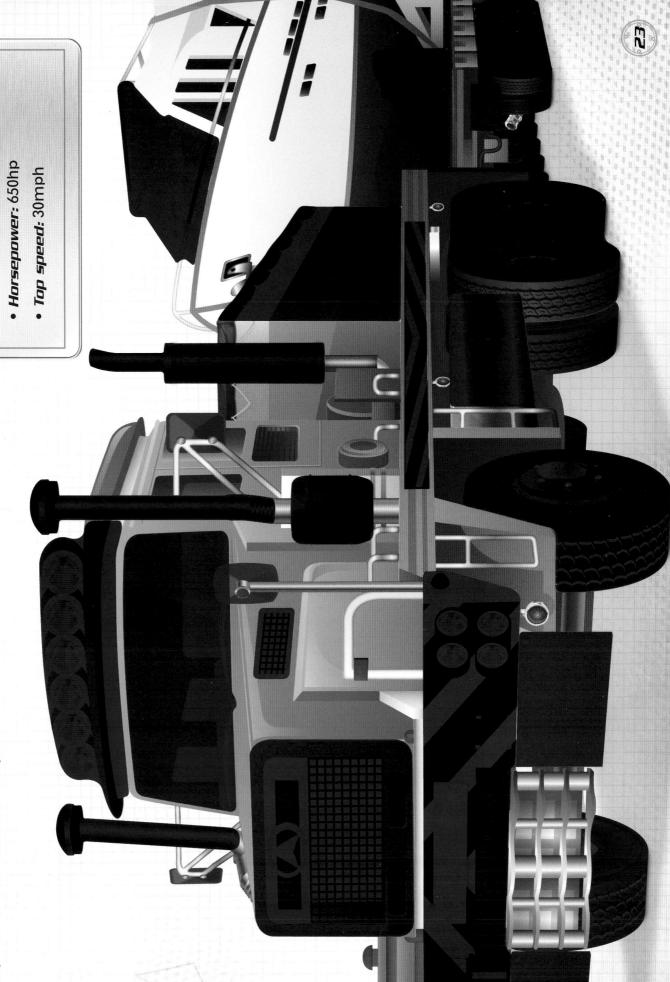

Glossary

- **ballast tractor:** a truck that pulls very heavy loads. It has a powerful engine, and extra weight over its back wheels to increase grip.

- **de-icing fluid:** a liquid that melts ice and snow

- **drag race:** a short race down a straight track

- **dragstrip:** a straight racetrack, usually 400m long

- **horsepower (hp):** the power an engine is producing per second. The number in the statistics box is the maximum power that engine can produce.

- **hydraulic:** powered by liquid pressure

- **km/h:** kilometres per hour

- **loaded weight:** the weight of a fully-loaded truck

- **mph:** miles per hour

- **pickup:** a truck with no roof over its back end

- **pro-jet:** a truck that's been modified for drag racing

- **supercharged:** a vehicle with an engine that uses compressed air to create more power

- **tungsten:** a very tough metal, often used to make drills

Digital manipulation by Keith Furnival

Edited by Sam Taplin

RECOVERY

MO56 FGH

OVER

SIZE

NEXT 20 miles

6523-862

✱ These are extra stickers. Stick them wherever you like!

Armored truck page 4

SWAT

Construction dump truck page 5

UB36

⚠
Danger
Men at work

UB36

✳ These are extra stickers. Stick them wherever you like!

Fire truck page 6

NC7 YL39

Crane truck page 7

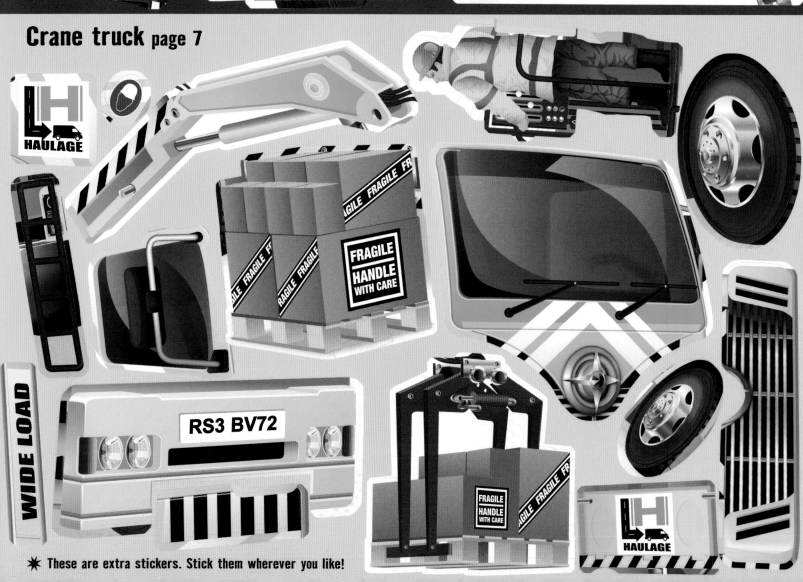

LH HAULAGE

WIDE LOAD

RS3 BV72

FRAGILE HANDLE WITH CARE

LH HAULAGE

✷ These are extra stickers. Stick them wherever you like!

EAGLE HAULING

G6283

*These are extra stickers. Stick them wherever you like!

Army truck page 10

ARMY

ARMY

SERGEANT WALKER
653-245-668
2ND BATTALION

35628-5

35621-5

Monster truck page 11

SMASH!
CRASH!

33

MONSTER TRUCKS

✹ These are extra stickers. Stick them wherever you like!

Suction excavator page 12

WASTE DEPT.

DANGER

CAUTION : SUCTION

Steam truck page 13

FINEST QUALITY WELSH COAL

COAL

FINEST MORGAN & SONS QUALITY

23

Flatbed dump truck page 14

McKEWEN CIVIL ENGINEERING

B520 3MG

✱ These are extra stickers. Stick them wherever you like!

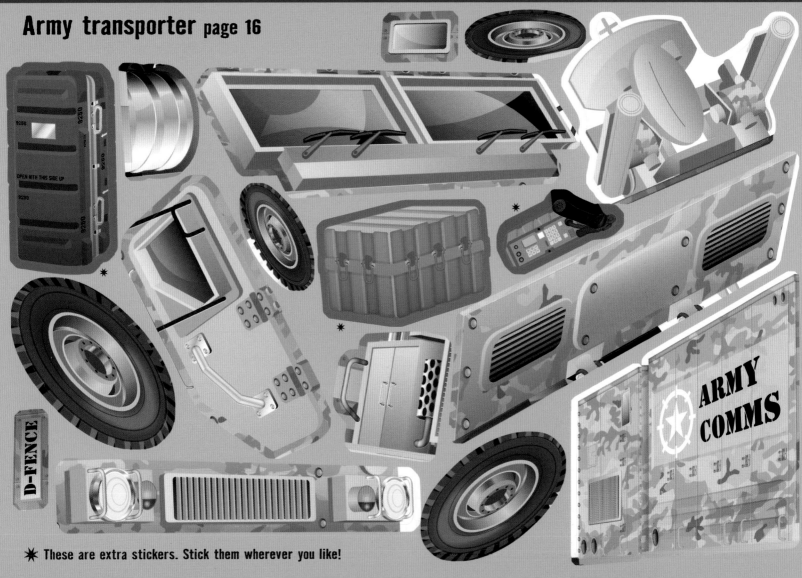

✳ These are extra stickers. Stick them wherever you like!

Vintage pickup truck page 18

CEMENT

CEMENT

MMC57

Buffalo Builders

Est. 1950

✷ These are extra stickers. Stick them wherever you like!

Concrete mixer page 19

Fuel tanker page 20

I ERGEX PETROLEUM CORPORATION

ENERGEX

MAYG 613

3Y
1863
WARNING

Pro-jet truck page 21

 These are extra stickers. Stick them wherever you like!

Snow plow page 22

90

90

Ballast tractor page 23

B449 BYT

SIZE

Seafarer

OVER

✱ These are extra stickers. Stick them wherever you like!